AF324321

PRECINCT KALI
&
THE GERTRUDE SPICER STORY

Other Books by James Bertolino

Employed, Ithaca House, 1972
Soft Rock, Charas Press, 1973
Making Space For Our Living, Copper Canyon
Press, 1975
The Gestures, Bonewhistle Press, 1975
Terminal Placebos, New Rivers Press, 1975
The Alleged Conception, Granite Publications,
1976
New & Selected Poems, Carnegie-Mellon
University Press, 1978
Are You Tough Enough For The Eighties?, New
Rivers Press, 1979

Precinct
Kali

&

The
Gertrude
Spicer
Story

Poems by
James Bertolino

Photography and Graphic Design
by Lois Bertolino

New Rivers Press 1981

Library of Congress Catalog Card Number: 81-80548
ISBN 0-89823-034-9

Typesetting by Peregrine Cold Type
Book Design by C. W. Truesdale and Lois Bertolino

Acknowledgments:
Thanks to the editors of the publications where many of these poems first appeared: *California Quarterly, Casaba, Chiaroscuro, Cincinnati Poetry Review, Clifton, Epoch, Gegenschein Quarterly, Granite, Gumbo, Ironwood, Jeopardy, La Fusta, Live Writers, Moosehead Review, Occurrence, The Ohio Journal, Orion Press, Paintbrush, The Painted Bride Quarterly, Partisan Review, The Penny Dreadful, Poetry Now, Porch, Rainy Day, Sou'wester, Star-Web Paper, Stinktree, Stooge, Telephone, Vegetable Box, Waters* and *Yardbird*.

Some of the poems in this volume are reprinted from *Terminal Placebos*, 1975, New Rivers Press; *Are You Tough Enough for the Eighties?*, 1979, New Rivers Press; and *The Alleged Conception*, 1976, Granite Publications—Copyright © 1975, 1976, 1979 by James Bertolino.

Precinct Kali & The Gertrude Spicer Story has been published with the aid of grants from the Arts Development Fund and the National Endowment for the Arts and with the help of the Charles Phelps Taft Memorial Fund, University of Cincinnati.

Special thanks to Elise Smith and Roberta Rigsby for the turtle shells.

New Rivers Press Books are distributed by
    Small Press Distribution, Inc.   and   Bookslinger
    1784 Shattuck Ave.   330 East 9th St.
    Berkeley, CA 94709   St. Paul, MN 55101

PRECINCT KALI & THE GERTRUDE SPICER STORY has been manufactured in the United States of America for New Rivers Press, Inc. (C. W. Truesdale, editor/publisher), 1602 Selby Avenue, St. Paul, MN 55104 in a first edition of 750 copies of which 15 have been signed and numbered by the Bertolinos.

"It was not by making yourself heard but by staying
sane that you carried on the human heritage."
—*George Orwell*, 1984

"You can call this 'Collected Bertolino' if you like,
but only in the sense that it brings together for the
first time in one large volume a strain of American
poetry that is very rare—a virus, a genius, a
madness—that looks at what we are in this country,
and laughs. There is no do-it-yourself utopianism
here, no romantic solutions, no nostalgia or
illusions, nothing that looks or smells like the
American Dream, and no effort to teach us to be
better and more compassionate human beings. His
gift, simply, is to make us see in hundreds of ways
what we are and to cause us laughter and
recognition. He is our Fool and Trickster, and we
are all his kings and queens."
—*C. W. Truesdale*

Precinct Kali
& The Gertrude Spicer Story

Terminal Placebos

Are You Tough Enough For the Eighties?

Specific Collisions

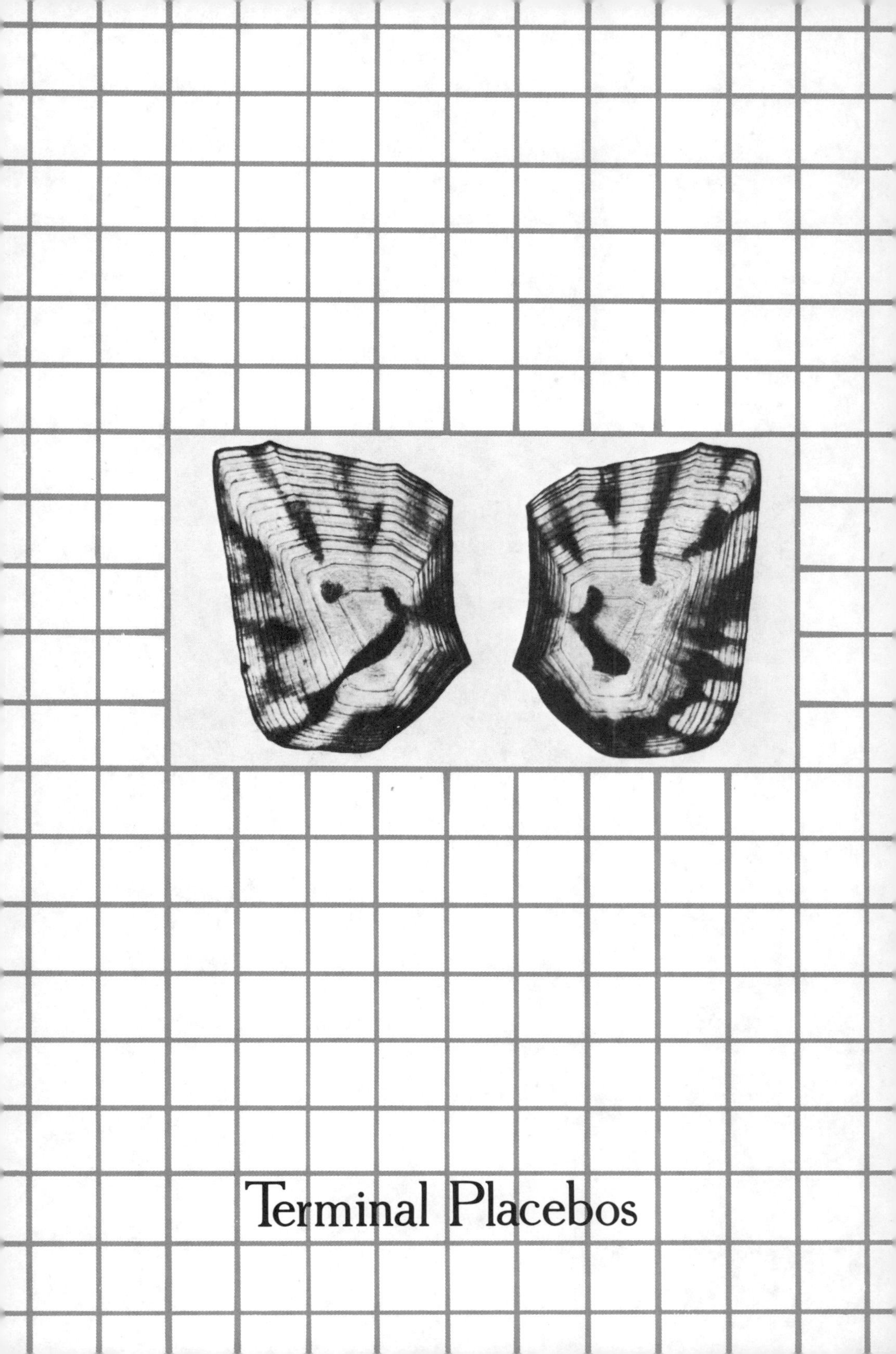

Terminal Placebos

The Shovel

You should have brought
the shovel
back. You know
we have trouble here.
The water's taken ill.
Your mother weeps her nights away
too. She fills our lunch sacks
with last week's rain.
And a kind of blue wart has killed
the peonies. It's your
backyard. The sand-box
is failing—your father drank the sand.
You should have come home.
We need the shovel
Jack.

The Will

To Bernice of
the graceful pauses
I leave my metal crutches.
To her guppy
a bit of tripe.
My pulling out alive
will remain for Charles, his wife will have
my softest wen. And to the University,
where mother came to bone,
the jellied hum.
The aliquot of slaughter
will stroke the children to weep
for translucence.
To them I leave the crate.

Lament For Julep

Born of bafflement
before the ways we turn
to nothing,
born of substantial parents.

Calf-raffle. Baby's Breath.
Referenda gone berserk.

We loved you Julep.

Herd-weak & lost
to density cursing mass—you've left
our space
a blind hole
that's all of you &

sucks at us.

Petroglyph: A Veneration

*" . . . because all books are dead
and we live where the edges
overlap."*
—Tom Raworth

The automated petroglyph
still hides
below the Zen Master's robes,
weaving & bobbing
like a small rubber palm.

The automated petroglyph renews,
shedding listless caterpillars
onto our tents. Tomorrow
something yellow
must die.

The automated petroglyph returns
to the Chapel of Painful Submission,
its vestigial muscles
thinking hemlocks
throughout the suburbs.

The automated petroglyph
kissed
for its pure
oscillation,
sticks like grass
to the top of our heads.

Archetypal Protocol

Enormously at variance
with the mule's earache
& feeling precocious

she drew a picture
of testes flattened
between bricks. Knowing

full well the
aborigines
can't read, we flattered her

with studied leers
& led her toward
the "pit".

All twelve of us hummed
the familiar melody
of "Lost in the Vagina"

as she gestured cosmic-
ally, clawed
the air & fell.

Camping Out

1

Mrs. Drew tends
to be a little strange
anyway. She talked
all night
of something she called
metaphysical couvade
& the bulldog
cylinder.
Not one of us
understood
though she demonstrated
with a trowel.

2

Henry, maybe thinking
of what she said in
the tent, & hoping we'd look
to him for the giggle
slipped into
the creek &
shrieking lyrical abstractions
tore his trousers.

3

She reeled
fighting
for thigh-bound spirituality,
his genteel gore.

Ontological Pornography

They made it in a tent
on a parking lot.
"We are animals in rut"
said Christine-the-slimmer.

Do unto your bumpers & grids,
do the macadam.

Lifting the coverlet
he allowed that chilly breezes
might wrinkle the scrotum.
Prepuce expansion.
Oh cock.

Oh Avis it Hertz!

1) Inventing the canvas fold-out
& rental sex-pack.
2) Preventing life on the highways.

"You bell my clapper" he sang.

3) A quaint church
nestling
in paved foothills.
4) Denying orgasm for reasons
too painful.
5) Applying physics to flesh.

We'll park our bodies
& find true sex
beyond the sweat & thrash
of the particle universe

we'll feather the waves
& make babies
in reverse.

Metaphysical Bum-Sonnet/1

A green plastic stamen
is the key!
Twist the appleskins taut, tie
the epidermal foil
to your foreknobs.

Once critical speed is reached
your mother's menses
a kind of slippery ballad,
a Law degree or
something Alyce takes off on stage.

Let traditional metrics
rage. Pollen-dipped drumsticks
poached for brunch.
Look for a fence-post to rob.

For Claire Levenhagen

Metaphysical Bum-Sonnet/2

Don't balk at the red owl,
it eats mushrooms too.
Deep behind its face
the inscrutable swims
for its life. Because it is

it means. Because it is no longer
the opaque window sings.
Don't balk at change.

A sermon encased in glass
whirrs out of steam &
we gather to hum its praises.
Precious droplets of common moisture
form a liberating chain.

A feathered forehead, a damp cowl.

For Robert Morgan

Circle-Jerk

My ass is a temple she croaks.
So does a frog, & there's more
to an empty wine bottle.
She likes to shout down freights.

She calls her coupling
the boogie fuck. Put a cork in her mouth
& she'll let go a few flats. Poems
like this are circle-jerks, they

jerk & circle, jerk & circle.

Her confessor swoons. My ass
is a miracle! A miracle
my ass, three Hail Marys & an Our Father for you.

She steals his sacred juices
& breaks wafer for good.

Untoward Rose

Bespectacled & prim.
Where in the backhoe legend
will we market this simple

disaster? A summer wasted on weed
is more than a professor.
A trick-baby striped like morality
on an orgy of rosewater. I said backhoe.
Cat. Rotorooter bliss

comes to college. Lets get
your 2nd grade nun into this.

Cross-masturbation. The universe
like a beehive. We'll spin the grim reaper
to a tight weave, chaste.

Bountiful Acne

The peace-creeps are balling
the grunts. Here's
the old-fashioned blessing
for our lunch. The universe is chaos
& we're blind
to the hole in the shadow

of the cross
winds. So like
easing back to consciousness

this simple glider. From this high
the clumps of tiger-lilies a good case of acne
rampant through the fields. Don't

lullaby me you skinny stiff, I want meat!

No tantrum of genius will forsake
brute fuck.

The Dangerous Immaculate

Good & Evil, you think
of your married friends
who really dislike each other,
aren't good for the children
seem wrong you say think of
the universe as a kind of beehive
but no, they have this vow

& John Ashbery
an expressionist landscape
the form everything seems to lean toward
the longer you look

She says "fuck you!"
He says "I'd like to"
& arches humming into his

The dangerous tomato
The immaculate

The Miraculous Tangerine

You take my fingers
& my elbow, my
scrubbed foreknob
into the Chapel of Tangerine.

You take me. My schoolbooks
askew in the damp grass
like so many stream pebbles.
You loosen the burnoose, a ripple
down my flank.

We drink. We receive
the citrus blessing a fruity
punch. Doubling over
in the position known to induce

I club you to death.

The Surgeon

The tree surgeons did
what they do
made love with their chain saws
till you could stand no more
& left me here alone
yammering like a calf

I glisten with their immaculate killing

They've gone
& the leaves I sleep on
decorate my buttocks
with their veins

My penis rose like a tree
I cut it

please forgive me

Hummingbird

So delicate a word
we fear the child.

You cling to your past
where your mother waves the blue kerchief

your earlobes flail, no no no
inert
beneath belief.

O love
our basement sinks

no colloquy can save us

you touch my cornea with your tongue
& we read of it.

The Release

Adrift in a vision of mountain tunnels
trucking in the Rockies.
Loads of logs.

Your grandmother knew molasses
& your shoe,
the old one you used for packing-in your sorrows.
But the way they lifted off
slowly, with a vibrating hum
high into the thin, cold air

you felt cheap. You wept.

Drifting now a bloody knothole
in a suicide plan,
your fingers un-
clasp, releasing the only love she grew.

Prostate Charisma

From his hospital bed he says
I miss the boar-grunt blessings,
dung on the wind. My chest
is tits & still they give me
needles. I remember

the old country. I know
dirty pictures in the attic
whack-off the teenager. What else
could I do? Too much

real butter. Suppositories
are no treat. The nurse picks off
the sheet & says she'll pray
for my body. Who needs that?

Some Lines for MFA Writers Wherever They May Be

All anguish is theoretical,
wild saliva.
Who spit blood in the Jujubes?

Brandy starts the new stance
below the addiction
threshold. We lay together

to break a moan.

This is about requited love &
the feasible orgasm
which happens

here.

Don't say this is
the beginning
of a writing career. Don't say
career. These lines
are not "another matter"

& we don't mean to rhyme.
So take your terror straight
& pick out the cotton
left by
the headphones.

Juice it.

It's the Muse staring through
like a laser sizzling a retina
brings us to an off-rhyme in home.
Brings us to drool
for crucifixion.

A sexual allusion to Krapp's last spool.
An erection of comfort.

The desire to end this
with something beautiful
is a kind of rape.

Garden Smack

This is garden smack,
this is America.
This isn't Molasses University.
We're not in Kansas.

This is where it takes a knife in the back
to get dignity
between the lungs.

It's all a matter of re-entry speed
& pressed pink wafers
of fusil oil & blood.

Even the Great Leaders wake from their Dreams
with r.e.m. hardons.

They're after us pal.

They're not frogs
going gribbitz gribbitz in the mud—
they're swinging spades
toward our gardens, hankering

for cock & balls
the body's wrinkled tubers.

For Tyler Fleeson

Terminal Placebos/1

People do the weirds for more
money & fame than
church control

Rate your loved one

Ow that smirks

& Christine still in love
with internal medicine
how painful the failure of that concern

Dildo slick as a skeeter's tongue

Wheels across space touching
lightly, lifting from
the nerve knot below the neck's base
your stone

Never trust a jesus freak's placebo

Terminal Placebos/2

Half the brains it took to survive
the Om tomb

Rate your lobe

Sucking the artificial limb

In control
utterly
& weeping by turns

We acknowledge its pain but must
continue meeting microbes
openly

A fistful of nightsoil reconstitutes the academy

Subtle
as litmus revolt

Terminal Placebos/3

Bending slightly she
overcame
the spheroid desperation
of a certain memory

Post-coital political struggle

& after the rise of
clitoral criticism
we pass the bladder signal

Death as pleasure field

Toward resurrection of slaughtered intelligence
as machismo prayerwheel

We're gamey, tough
at center,
declare communal pulse-rape
a natural holiday

Terminal Placebos/4

We took him in & waited
for them to show
but he didn't last so we left

Presidential tumescence

Today in France
a cluster of seven unemployed bishops
consecrated the eleven-
inch erection
of a thalidomide adolescent

Evincing the anal control of a Quaker mutant

Disguised as waning faith in natural foods

We applaud the lesser fortune
spent bugging
the perfect masters of psychic adultery &
assassination techniques

Catharsis outlaws
doing time in the Ivy League

Terminal Placebos/5

The history of foreign policy
as hard-core pornography

Post burial menopause blues

Received four years to life
for dealing
in TM techniques, outlawed
by the Unlimited Realities Act

Bending to pick a blossom she notices
the fear

The rate at which the peripheries
of human consciousness expand
is conversely proportional
to the increase in density of the black tumor

Father, your finger up me, is that grace?

Terminal Placebos/6

Sleeping through a seminar
on the mock-hormonal flow
of Papal securities
his hard-on
gradually supplanted attention

But lieutenant, human lives are priceless

If we cut which side'll get the tube?

The beauty of nuclear waste
as a kind of immortality for the species

Gloria disappeared when the media
broke her coverage of executive decree
administered to House & Senate as
"the usual double-blind procedure"

America practices anal rape abroad

She's crazy
but she's got a system

Terminal Placebos/7

Pondering the supreme world
of surfaces made of space

Learning to lie eloquently

Their meeting the
astral orgasm of two spheres, skin
of each touching at all points
a portal

Cross-cultural worship of stasis

Cross-channel cunnilingus as political tool

Our famous appalachian wart collection
his pay-off for bombing bathrooms
in the International Centre
for Ambidextrous Masturbation

Famous for salad festers

The academy discovers
the coherence of velocity

Surgery

I ain't no dildo
illiterate
she said. I've suffered
the terminal perversity of acupuncture
& love's ruin—

its mystical ash.

Once past the initial frictions
I can turn a sack
of blood garbage
into a sweet little tune.
It's the proscription of sextuplets
I'm for

& pleasure's anesthesia.

French Kiss

Her tongue in
my cleft
palate
a finger playing
the ridge

she kill for pleasure
she not a zoo-baby &

there's a ravine behind
my dead grandfather's mortar-
chinked log barn
where I lost the double-barrelled
gun that shot corks

& dirt into her eyes
she cried
I couldn't let her go she'd tell
her mother

threw it in the crick
I didn't lose
my way back over the baby toads
ankle-deep
that year

I lied they didn't
like my nose
mouth I talk funny &
hate
your tongue you slut

The Artificial Limbs Club

Last week I talked
on poetry
for the artificial limbs people.
I floored questions.
They came around
flexing their fixtures, the sunlight
off polished metal
pulling the walls in.

I said a small poem you command,
the large has you in
for tea & locks the door.
What I said waned in importance
as I gained charm.
A musk grew I was
a buck goat fluttering my tongue
for a kiss.

There was Jeanette
whose fingers
& forearms were nude.
In her eyes was an intelligence
surrounding the room.
They worshipped her
& my presence was what they did to congregate.

I came to talk & they said write
for us a poem about her.
We've let you see.

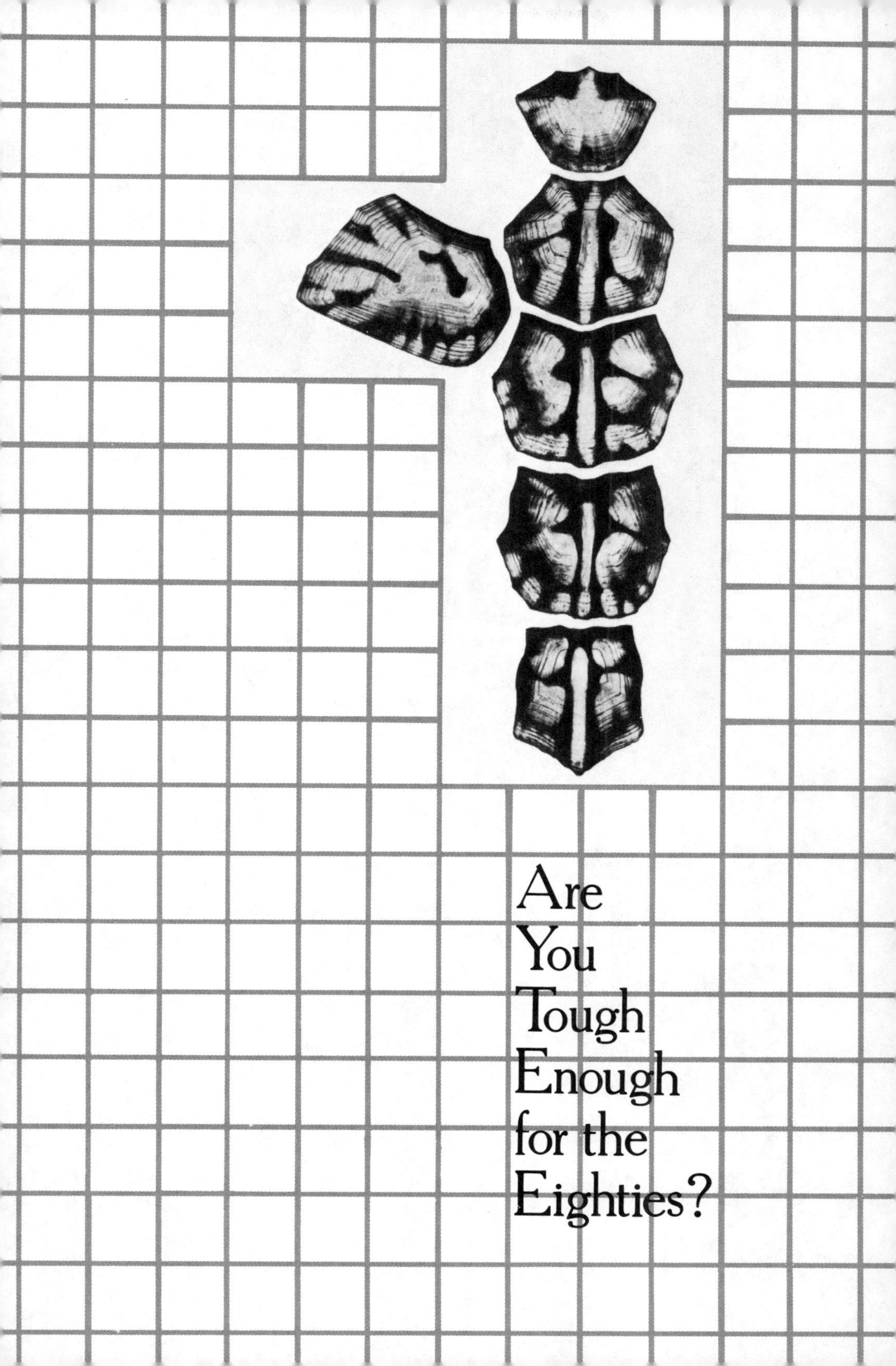

Are
You
Tough
Enough
for the
Eighties?

1980

Okra and bean sprites played riot
with domestic spaces

while terrorists rubbed plutonium
into the dry folds of recession. Votes

were cast, and before the mantle of persuasion
fell on its feces

a wizened Sufi surrounded the pile.

Earthworms went on strike
for safer loam.

Syllables followed like ill ducklings
a feather down stream.

Killer Chemicals

Russellville, Ky. (UPI)

A chemical detergent
spray was
dropped on millions
of blackbirds in
a 29-acre roost
last night

Snow flurries were mixed
with light rain
and temperatures in the
upper 20's as a cold
front moved through
the area—perfect

Conditions to allow
the detergent to wash
protective oils from feathers and
temperatures cold enough
to let the birds die
of exposure

Letter From Puerto Rico

A fine morning
to you.
Things are
shaping up for me
over here. I am thinking
of getting back into
Ham Radio. My job
is pretty good. Weather
here has been quite
changeable. Those pictures
are nice. You can get prints
you know. I'm thinking of
having one on my desk—
to remind me of our
"funny sides." I think you
should know I'm doing
better with my problem now.

The Abortion

In the study, near the bed, near
the blackened bootstring's
constellation of knots,
the old cat lies pulling at
her stitches. Already the fresh

bleeding has mixed with the orange
of antiseptic. Already the wound
has become hers. Now her sharp tongue

probes for the tumor, that comforting lump
she knew as a kitten. But no, her last
chance to nurse and clean
has been taken, and now her slow
body shivers, her head goes down.

Modern Lives

1.

Late Mother

Her face
a crutch
on ice

her thoughts
deranged as
a shattered hip

she comes forward
to touch
the infant's
genitals

with the cool
metal
of her spoon

2.

Brilliance

Take the deaf
mute whose
eyes are twin stars
of pain.
Brilliant.

Take the country-
western singer.

Take the boy who wasn't
asleep
when mother

conceived his enemy.
Brilliant.

Take the billiant news
of cancer,
of car-wreck at
36 below. Take the love's chain-
saw in the limbs.
Home.
God's brilliance.

3.

The Love

Six
mysteries
the brush of
her hip

indictments
the push-
pull of
her breathing
in his room

I love you she
once said but
this makes
my heart
vomit

4

The Lover

You hurt her
with your hard
body and then

you stopped her cold.

The rains took
her face
down the creek

old badger
praised her bones.

5.

The Loss

Love loss:
a brownish
paste
or the word
dysfunction

your future
coming on

a pick-up truck
driven into
the ditch
to kill a dog

The Coach

He teaches the boys
and girls to play
volleyball and soccer.
He has the large
engine in his car,
which is fast,
loud, and silver.
Today the red-
head Hollywood star
is coming to the shopping mall,
coming with her
slippery oscar.
He wants to slide his
butcher knife
between her ribs.
His tiny penis
was eaten by
a rat in his crib.

The Burden: A Ballad

The one tear she
shed for me
still limps home
with its burden of neon light

and I am bored in life
awaiting the sudden

The Big Rig

Gonna learn to drive
the big rigs, gonna learn
to fly.

I been hanging here
since I was a kid, not
getting someplace, just getting pushed
around. I never much liked
this town, never liked the people.
I'm tired of trouble, tired
of being scared to kick ass.

Gonna get me a rig and make some cash.
Gonna set the record straight.

The Nice Guy

You there

    Middle-aged man
    in green work shirt
    pants
    work shoes
    with a dented gray lunch box
    under your arm
    stepping off
    that bus

      you catch my eye
for a moment
        don't
look away
    in you rests
    a commitment
    of mine

here
    let me carry your lunch box

you needn't know me and
you don't
      but listen
      I know you have a daughter
      who takes lessons
      on the violin   you work
      evenings
      tending bar to pay for them
      don't you

sure

and your wife has four brothers
all of them bigger
than you
play poker   throw horseshoes

right

          but you don't
          really like them
          do you
                    that's okay
                    really

I know how it is
I know a lot
about you
          you're a nice guy

mind your business
just want to be left
alone

I'm going to kill you

The Wellness Conference

She repeated for us
all she knew of
the amputee issue.
The bliss is untenable
she said, and spoke of a swarm
that complicates the tongue.
Avoid stray marks and corner rust.
Revive the hunger for cost.

We learned then our one decision
is made by grief-light,
and as we toasted the new
gangrene paste procedure,
her face became
the exquisite wound.

Health Care

She is subject to toad
faints
the Doctor claimed.
His research in oral malfunction
led quickly to the mauve
fricative and

the buttery gleam
of tragedy.

The ward went ragged
to the moan of
let me be your bomb shelter baby . . .

Not too late for shock-tuning
and hormone
reversal. Too soon
for solar power. Profits

will suffer, wailed the Chief. Give me

health care that sharpens
the human, give me
an elegant cry
of despair—nothing better!

Jelly-Bean Jewelry

Somebody consumed
the jelly-bean jewelry.
The black went first,
then those with tender green sprouts.
We must feed the world's wealthy, yes,
but is it Art? Will China realize
a handsome return? And how does Christianity
figure in this? Some fiend,
starving no doubt, ate our beans
without preference for color
or creed. But the black
went first,
we know that.

The Politician

Even his armpits
are going bald.

In the corner of his mouth
the white fleck
of speaker's spittle
has been applied with make-up.

His face in the elevator
is a drainage ditch

and his asshole squeaks.

Questions For Quitting No. 4

Who laughed
longest
when the bright
young
Senator from
Nevada
pitched
the Siamese
kitten
and string of lit
cherry-bombs
into the broom
closet?

Yellow

No idea but
her penis

perfume

eyelashes butterflies settling
to eucalyptus

whispering

his breath
catches

and slips

The Professional

You claim the poem
about water
that came when you pulled
flesh back at the sink

When you pulled your trousers on
you chose not
to identify the weeping

We'll be good friends
you answered
turning your back
turning a little red in the face

One's work makes demands

No need to defend
a commitment
to grace

No shame your
infernal genius for pain

Could You Walk Out?

If someone close
to your mother
said "I feel amphibious"
and your father came out
of retirement to
break that person's cartilage

If your younger sister
displayed suddenly
and no one in the family could speak

Would bottom-fish attack a skunk?

Could you walk out of your limbs
and survive?

The Alps

It happens I'm dying
of this language.
I have become the lost
climber in the chilly
post-literal alps.

So high in the body the blood thins.

To survive I must be as intimate
as oxygen.

The Epic

Starting with an emotion
inexpressible
as fear suffered
by a domestic animal, or hope
that the twentieth century will end.

A hotel falls into the ocean.

How can we tell what we feel?

Easter, 1979: A Litany

Let us praise desperate repetition

the crone's worry beads
in an earthquake

the strings of dried mouths
about the necks
of the elegant Exxon wives

Let us praise bankrupt technology

the fingers of corruption
opening the dikes
of nuclear disease

Let us praise the church of born-again profit

Let us praise the politicians and polluters
for they are instruments of God

Let us praise televised armageddon
for we will suck poison
and destroy our young

The Balloon Of No Karma

Adrift in a haze of information,
the goat-footed turtle waits.
Nearby, dolphins invent topologies,
gorillas make signs and mute spiders
exchange epics of chemical speech.
Everywhere the organelles are chanting.

The managers and mystics are copulating.
The college of cardinals has targeted cancer
and the terrorists have employed T.M.
The curators bear arms and the sun
drums cadence to Jupiter's snake dance.

Now rising, heavily, like the crystal-centered
boulder gravity failed, like the balloon
of no karma with a small-eyed grin,
the red-faced genius mongoloid has come.
The way is simple, simple, we are saved.

To William Irwin Thompson

Turtle Song

I am the goat-footed turtle.
My house is four and my feet
are three—the cloven.
I swim with the porpoise,
walk with the snake and deer
and I climb. I am the genius mongoloid.
I have come to lead you
to the new world.

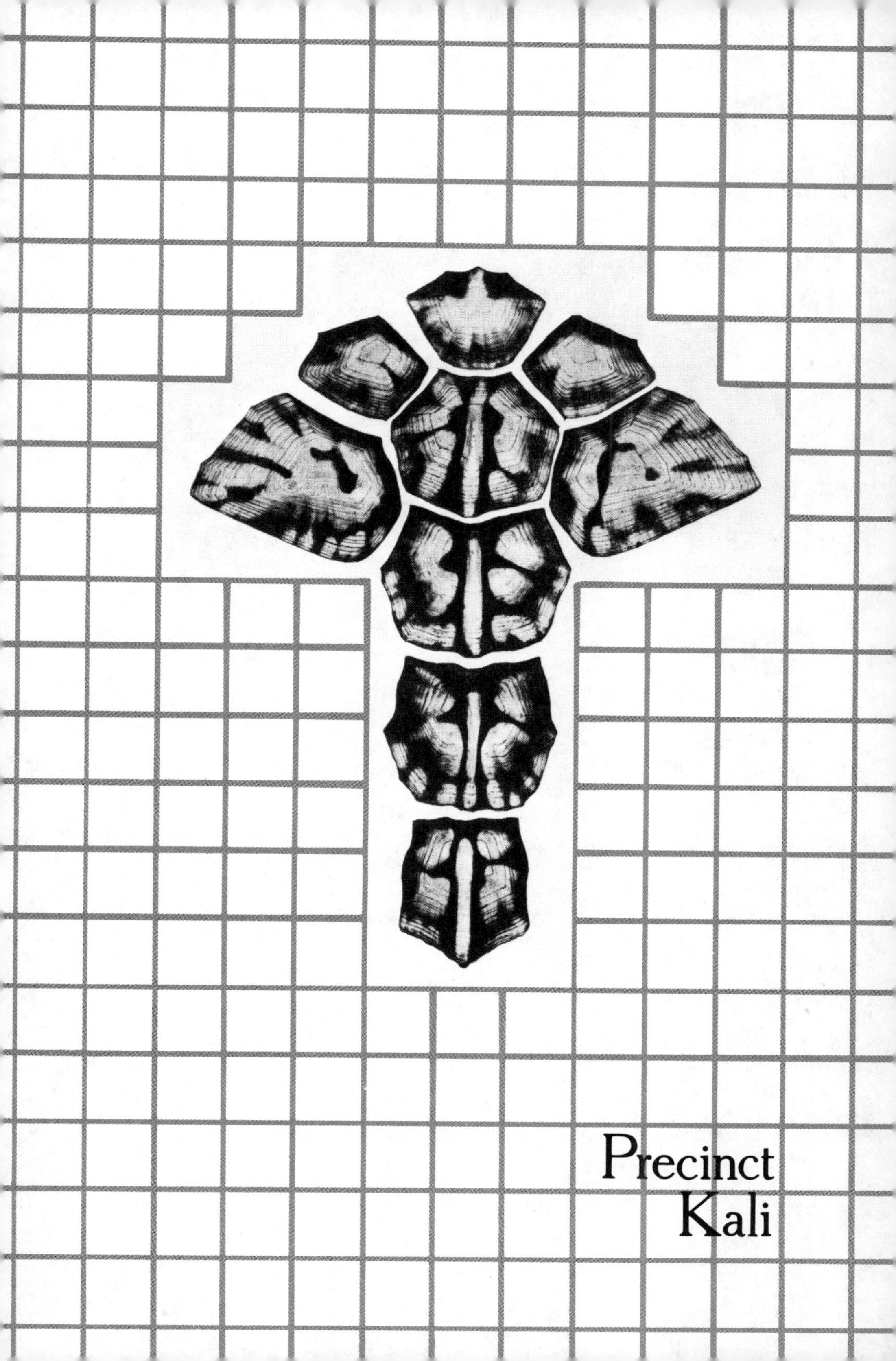

Precinct
Kali

The Library

I am Harry Truman
& have hurt you more than
you can know

it was my accent
my harmless collection
of Avon bottles
they are cancer climbing stairs
in your bones

I have founded research
there will be no need to keep dying
on television
& in the churches
no need to eat chemicals

all my breaths have been flattened
like Picasso portraits

please, I beg you, move amongst them
through my library
on the track we have provided for your health

You will forgive me & come to no harm.

A Walk With Codrescu

Not far behind his yurt
where we moved
in a crouch
through the complicated greenery

where a slight breeze caused
sunlight to jabber at us
like a strobe

we heard the last rustlings
of bathroom noise &
noticed signs of feminine itching.

We discussed the area as a proper site
for yoga, then sealed
with bean-curd
our ear holes.

We carried with us four dark rooms.

The Eleventh Hour Poem

Time to think of rodents
in Mesopotamia, & the yellow
Studebaker the girls broke
their bones over. There's a prize-
fighter in the Pastor's future,
alfalfa sprouts rafting
the melted cheese.

We form a committee to host
the second coming of
synchronicity. We ponder swelling
at the joint & the magic
of ear calves. Logic
is the formal accident we
will have no part in.

Citrus vermin & land crabs
have civilized a native
called Mordant. A shill. A stretch
of reason cuter than vinyl
veneer. We've earned our genitals
& class them fiction. We thumb
rides in the Satori wheelchair.

Sparrows

We happened on a burst
of brick music
36 inches from the yellow.
Adrian spoke in layers there
& to this day will
not compute. To some

the *brick symphony*, to others
lemon concertina
makes sense & goes
the distance. How convince
the family this talk
is not symptomatic? We care

for sincerity. We carefully
dismount the space craft.
Bereft. Be wary of
baloney boats & the Spring toad-count.
Be worthy of your name.
You are full, you are

64 sparrows & spilling.

Chakra Steps

First reclaim
the small
blue mouth
at the base of the spine

Then plant passion
beneath the landscapes
of protein

Now climb the steps
of semen
to the brain

Precinct Kali

She was the ground
for a no hint pass,
& she liked being that.
It was bugging a boulder
she'd say, or being a turtle
in a quarry.

She strangled an oak once
and though indicted
still got the bonus.
I can't live with this
her husband cried, she's a cloud
killer, & strings her

slavic grunt through my alphabet—
ain't a word in this house
don't leak! We took note
however, & reported him
the closet fog-racer. So she freed
us, took us off his case

with a suction so lethal
semen climbed the spine
& made thought translucent—
breath on a mirror.

The Post-Tantric Kite Fly

Let me put you in touch,
you've been too long
in the head.

Halve a melon, musk
or casaba,
then rest your elbows
in the frothy hollows
while studying
a photo
of your lover in nude.

This is position one
& imagined while bathing.

Now stretching the fingers
in direct sunlight,
you will notice shortly a tingling in the wrists
& a slight pinch at the juncture
of kite-string & ear.

Being more than a metaphor
behind astral travel,
you succeed position six.

What remains is curvature &
a parasexual organ
of etheric viscosity.
Let me put you in tongue.

The Dance We Learned

Remember our long afternoon of amusement
with their tantric computer,
the bent light and the liquids
where we found them? You seemed
alarmed. You spoke again of loss
and of the mucilage you valued as a child.
"The rubber tips made me think
of mother's nipples" you told me. You begged
that I forgive your debt.

It was like a dance we learned
by simply being where the music was.

The Cathedral

I'm an architect
& these thin struts
of consciousness
are my portfolio.

You know my work perhaps,
the benzene ring or
that black tunnel twisting
from Christ to last week.

But it's these small things
make my mother proud,
the indoor root system
for liquid waste &

the transparent hair-net.
I'm planning now for
a perpetual-thought
space sculpture: a reversing

biocosmic field I'll call
the Cheops Chakra Cloud.
I figure we might program it
to pray, or prove we exist.

The Institute

1

Coming around the bumper
of the lime green Maverick she
lifted her left shoulder and let out
a little whistle. Her feet were bare,
no 'crunch of the gravel.' Lamar sat in the lawn
chair, looking like his name. As she approached,
off the gravel onto the grass, her arms swung over her hips,
fingers doing a little air dance. Lamar coughed, sounding like a
small child, rose, and taking a long breath, slid his hand down the
front of her cut-offs. He grinned, 'hiya, Red.'

2

Leslie. We knew we had to figure the mathematics of the thing. We knew they'd be around any day looking for their money, and we had to be ready. Leslie was the answer. Six initiates a day was her average, and no repeaters. Sure, we used the honor system, she could be lying, but nobody doubted her abilities. She had left the Kundalini ashram after 16 astounding days—slicing the tomato in front of the assembled members was what finally did it. They all witnessed what poured out. She had to leave, she said.

3

Erick came back to the shop one Saturday morning, visibly disturbed. Apparently the clerk at the post office branch had warned him that the Postmaster was planning action against the 'Cosmic Light people,' for the 'porno' we'd been mailing, and that the non-profit privileges would be first to go. I called an emergency meeting that evening. We decided it must have been the promotional photos of our group massage program at St. Teresa's.

4

Getting the rifle and scope was a problem. To be safe, we had the rifle purchased at a sporting goods store in Kentucky, and the scope at K-Mart. We paid the buyers each $25—I don't know who they were. Red told us her friend Lamar could be trusted, that he'd been a sharpshooter, an assassin in the Marines.

5

Well, it worked. *Time* magazine is interviewing Leslie and me next week about her photographs. They are planning to call the feature 'The Death Aura.' Already enrollment at the Institute has tripled, and after the *Time* article comes out, who can tell? There will probably be enough demand to go national. Ground-breaking in Detroit is scheduled for April. Eric is running for City Council— if he wins, and he will, our local credibility will be impeccable. I'm proud of us all. The real work of Cosmic Light has just begun.

St. Irwin, The Martyr

Sorcerer, mutant, call him
what you will. He spoke of bird
funnels, and of the breathing mountains
before America drowned.
He described Earth's magnetic shells
as loose sheets of being, but the Pentagon
shot him down.

Memory is the backside of appetite
he taught us, we ingest the universe
with our forgetfulness. He said the door
to the world of surfaces swings in and
swings out with breath. It opens with breathing
and closes with our deaths.

Our bodies pay homage to the forms.

He wrote of sex as a ladder only two can climb.
His torturers remembered this
when they found him.
In the chapel to Nikola Tesla, which he built
of steady orbits at the age of twenty-three,
they suspended him on seven lasers
like a nude quail sizzling on a spit.
They jeered "wink out, you fool!"

But he was afraid, and fear is the black chute,
the nanosecond that never ends.
So he converted the pain and rode it out.

For C.W.Truesdale

The Gesture

Our room
a gesture
          freezes

the walls are cliffsides
the windows
             ash

a beauty gathers

& we breathe

we breathe to sing this fatal carol

Beauty is the butcher
whose lines

we croon

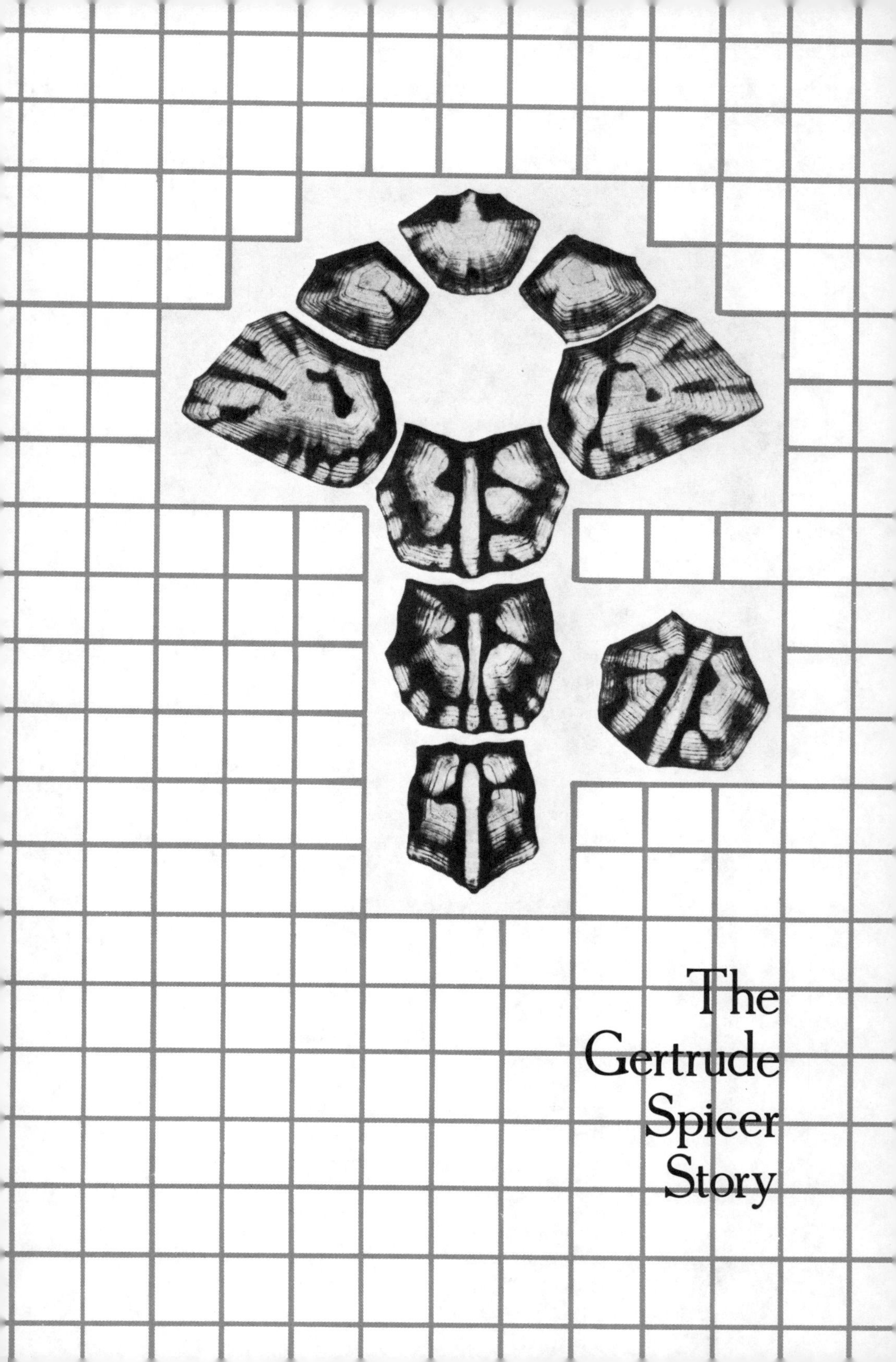

The
Gertrude
Spicer
Story

Not A Normal Tongue

Gertrude said the egg-carton
made me do it, that obscene,
that formed low-grade paper
caught me holding breakfast!

So we got our gear together
and drew conclusions. We wanted
music as chilling as the moan
of reason going down. That's

when Rudy said life is no
bowl of rose, and anyway,
I'm into forgetting. Forgetting
is three of my moves.

The Alien

The armature of her dismay survived
the disaster in Halifax.

It requires no polishing.

We've hung a proliferation of archaic verbs
like Christmas bulbs
along her tubes
and over the mesh-like grids. The effect

fragile as the idea of generation.

The Spectacle Of Orange

The spectacle of orange
fungus on a fallen
limb
brings back
her orangutan at Stonehenge,
the dancing, the
disturbing airs

The Exam

1. Restless as a fir tree in bra
& panties.
2. Hungry as postulates in drums
of drain oil.
3. Wizened freedoms.

Her exam was camping in Idaho.
Her prevalence was an old firearm.
Her curious neck spasm belittled
the marmots into outright attack.

She stripped quickly & slipped into a pond.
The dull foliage was smeared with midges.
The coyote lifted its leg &

delivered her baptismal name.

The Trunk Story

Undone by a towel on a tray.

No family to rush celery to the cistern
or dangle plums at floating cousins.

No surprise at finding Gertrude
with spiders
was our first advantage, her tiny engine
the last.

At our discovery of adolescence
described
in a burlap diary
Vernon gave in to a seizure.

We all screamed "Mexican virus!"

His sodden towel steamed like pork tripe.
Skin graft, navel, horse-hair bow.

The mules began to bray.

The Snails: A Novel

He was puzzled
and felt like glue
participating in the rich
daughter's melancholy.

Too late to pry her snails
from the beam.

Left Wisdoms

Never poke
yellow
she said

or resurrect
one's parents in
the clutch.

Stroke
midnight's cat tail
and remember

ease

is a blue valise of eggs.

The Stork Score

After they had settled comfortably
into the rhubarb cluster
she spoke at length
while he gave the honorary member
its strokes. he wondered what

had the peeled kielbasa
to do with the outhouse glee club?
What of the tongue garbage?

She produced at that moment the last
of the pickled sow's ear.
It was clear their session
had closed. She was done with diagrams
and made a move to cover herself
with several large leaves.

Her Monsignor

I propose this between
what the Monsignor saw &
the gala lobster luncheon.

She composed at brunch
then signed his contract.

The satin of her tunic was so fine
the elbow wound
spewed a brief chablis—clear,
& not without effervescence
in the mountain sunlight, the pure air.

Her tuba had no place, nor
the simple health of crab grass.

His growth, malignant, was buried
in the corn silk
behind her ear.

The Alleged Conception

Still sitting where Darrell took me
to watch jibberish grow wings

I don't feel like a sanitary landfill,
but I understand

her nerves were a basket of strings,
tangled slightly and swollen
with the milky stone

We bought a dead cloud
and stretched it out over the water bed

it got us all drunk and
now Gertrude's grown
a scrotum

come hook or crywater
I stand accused

The Bent Dream

Done with elbow wrestling
and still feeling fabulous
in the joints, she climbs over
the vegetable wreckage and proclaims:
I am the poem, I demand to be
the basket of flower eggs!

You're not a poem, he rags,
you're a busy virgin
hanging cartoon wallpaper
on an open marriage, and this
is a bent dream, a rubbery bone
I'll chew till noon!

Gertrude's Photos

So what if I stole your photos
of the president in bra and panties,
and fed your kitten carpet tacks,
I know you love me still—I helped
you get the grant. I twisted

knobs on the TV when your limbs
were sore. I inflated your tire.
I even stroked your body with
the phone while your mother sobbed
and begged you to speak. And remember

the swollen zucchinis and cucumbers
I pulled out of your drawers—they made me
feel so small. They endangered my career
in film, my mental health. Now you're
after my wealth, you say I owe you

for that operation. You claim the wart
grew back, but you don't have me fooled.
I know what you've been doing
with my hose, and so does your friend
Marlene. We think you are very strange.

Gertrude of the Stars

She let her hair down
to the immaculate hunger

to its dirty lisp.

My eyes are supernovae and
less gentle than

she said. I'm pretending
a dark astral pussy
and talk funny too. On the edge

of appetite
and more alone

she constructed as two
mouths tunneling
a model of the multiple universe.

The Gymnast

She let her hip slip past,
her pale wrists
rotating.

I'm no decoy
she spat,
a brush is a brush today.

And this is no religious
reverie
laced with sex
& science

this is dying fish
& crib death.

Our subscription has lapsed.

A Conversation

Gertrude said life is a decoy.
She said we need immersion
skills, need to know
the dreams of lichen, and the remote tickle
of symbiosis with a brick.

Still them, he shrieked, still your rife
shorebirds
before I'm moved to kill.

The Tallow Story

Out cruising for a piece
of the blame
they fell on a satchel
of stork tissue
and sold it

to a family of cistern claimants

Next they bought a bolt
of spider cotton
and employed it to entrap
a migrating
Mexican virus

A horde of piss crickets
jumped them
in an outdoor john, but Dolly
survived by pantomiming
her mother's
algae-ridden wooden bowl

Later she met a goat-footed turtle
who fitted her
for choke-mitts and quizzed
her thin syllable's
genitalia

Finally, after a meal of seltzer prunes
and potential tacos,
Dolly and the turtle guided a missle
of spleen tallow
toward the Vatican

demanding pitchblende
for Gertrude's bitter tendons.

The Bone Dowser

A leap of yodel
charisma
means more to the family
than auntie's gram of companionship.

We don't need drugs to remember the day
Gertrude married the bone dowser—it affected
our plans. Dad lost his business and Mom
took to scrawling "hornet paper" on church envelopes.
She licked the flaps and stuck them to everything,
including my tub raft, the woozy dutch elm and
the Mayor's fish tank.

Thankfully only Dad did time.

Thankfully several hours have passed.
Never mind the wheel chair, the floatation devices,
it's the buzzing in my marrow
that has my yodel slipping.

The Dowser

She went right and left at once
and we lost her. Never mind the new mattress,
it was a foul weather move, a play on our weakness.
Minutes have passed. The dowser's eyes claim
telling signals have begun to arrive. His rod
curves toward Venus. This is impossible, gripes Boris.
Next we'll be splitting photons. She's gone back
to the fuschia and there's nothing we can do.
The dowser nods and says he hears her giggling.

Specific Collisions

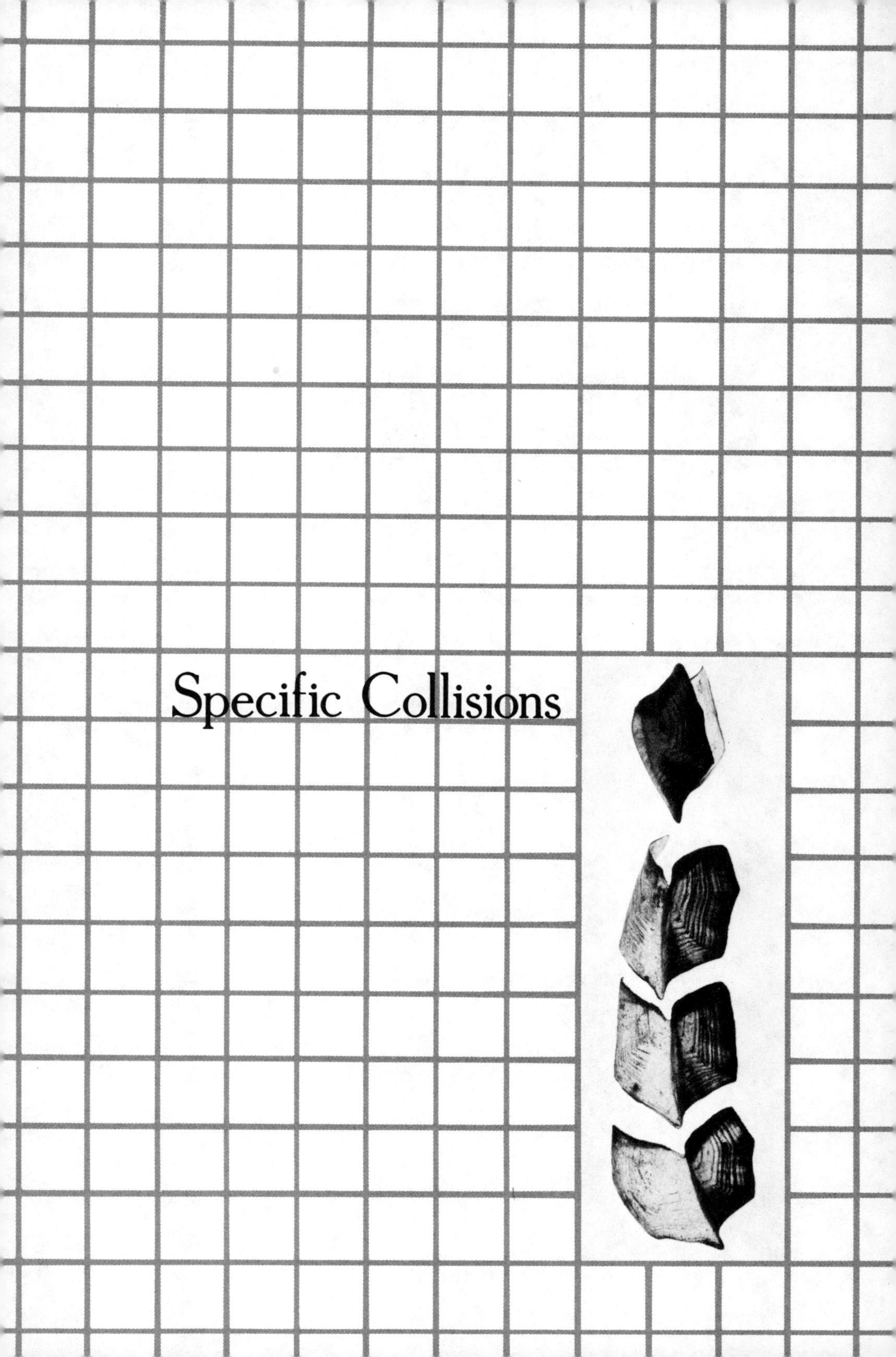

Specific Collision

Skateboard trauma stretches
before the student
like a massive jungle cat

There is fear, & an awe
as foreign as wax in the brain

Figures, these arrangements
let the back-mind speak
properly

where flesh exceeds

where word is instinct & design

The Sweet Potato

Consider the remote pleasures,
how they gather to invent

Remember when you trembled
for the last pear

Ask, if you will, that the sweet potato
explain itself

then prepare for the common thwart

No Discount

We've been pulling
tongue, unmasking
the automatic potato.

These collisions continue,
& our major pleasure
is alluvial.

So don't say this balance
isn't classical,
don't ride your truss

down teaspoon creek.
A stable of kinetic
nomenclature is not

a petting zoo. No discount
for fools.

The Damp Hammer

We drink the urban
potato
& dance
the pleistocene

Nothing soils us here

where the dampened
ball-peen
hammer

is a terminal theory of pleasure

or a swelling
in the dancer's feet

The Coupon Episode

Today we compare existentialism
to the Ph.D. Think colors,
the dusty squeaks.
Think as long as february
in the Rockies, deer water, glacier.

Or what does pewter share
with a lone ovum? When next
we write home for coupons
all depends on treble phrasing and
six-legged incest. Your mother
collects herself and squeals

"Don't be mouthy now you got
your degree!"

Tuxedo Neurosis

The small, brutal captives
have evolved as
our major
concern.

We thought their formal dress
a convenient
oppression

but now what approaches
like an oily fog
to threaten
this clinical delicacy

may be described only as
Freudness Peculiar—

the classic case of mongrel duty.

We must at all costs
crush this
surly convention.

They will not be rescued
by atrocities
of denim

or the disciplines of lust.

Midwest Olympics

1.
we felt dwarfed
by wrist worship

undone by a towel
on a tray

2.
No family of cistern
claimants

or strings of dawdle plums

no mute spiders
exchanging epics
of chemical speech

3.
It was the engine
advantage

the happiness
that rose by mid-day

like the Mexican virus

our perfect athlete
bound North
for the St. Louis entrail
slalom

The Sauerbraten Story

This is the story
of child greed
in the province of kohlrabi:

a crisis
of spinach fatigue.

We charged poetry with
diminishing
that young appetite
before a robbery of vegetables
took credence.

We knew seven syllables
could crush
a corn-oil rebellion,
& felt certain our honed lyric
would bridge
the sauerbraten abyss:

the lyric of yak fat
& the mud wolf,
of heavy petting & lungs
stunned by the long
slow moan
of dry leaves.

Poetry celebrates
the republic of meat.

The Vexing Questions

Some people hear the words
vegetable terminus
& think of pacific collision

or skateboard trauma

Some people are puzzled
why their families
survive

why Christmas at home is elitism versus mucus

As poetry is able, these lines
will answer the vexing questions:

how do we recognize the karma-looter

& will we be slain?

Cheese

I want to thank you for
the loaned lung
& for not pressing charges.

Karma-looting is no business
of the State.

Your friend, Sheriff Yellow
Kidney, though duly elected, is no
better than

the common thwart.

Please know that
more important than breathing
is the right to place
beaver
next to cheese.

For Tom Lux